T0123384

WRAPPED
—IN THE—
FATHER'S ARMS

The Role of The Father?

CHARLENE WARD

WESTBOW
PRESS®
A DIVISION OF THOMAS NELSON
& ZONDERVAN

Scripture taken from the King James Version of the Bible.

WestBow Press books may be ordered through booksellers or by contacting:

WestBow Press
A Division of Thomas Nelson & Zondervan
1663 Liberty Drive
Bloomington, IN 47403
www.westbowpress.com
1 (866) 928-1240

ISBN: 978-1-5127-4421-7 (sc)
ISBN: 978-1-5127-4420-0 (e)

Library of Congress Control Number: 2016908639

Print information available on the last page.

WestBow Press rev. date: 05/31/2016

Special Dedications

This book is dedicated to all the fathers and men who acted in the role of fathers. And a special thanks to my heavenly Father.

Heavenly Father,
When I was lost, You were so easy to find.
Little did I know, You were there all the time.
You showed me unconditional love in so many ways.
You gave me a new life, so I can be saved.
You are my father, my provider, my protector, and my comforter.
I can never doubt You, for there is no other.
So, I thank you, I praise you for who You are.
You may not be here in the natural, but I
know your love dwells in my heart.
And now, I respect and honor You, for
where You have brought me from.
I hope one day I will meet You and live in Your great kingdom.
Happy Father's Day.
Love, your daughter Charlene

Message from the Author

The information presented in this book is gathered directly or indirectly from life experiences. It is also based on the author's perspective as it relates to the scriptures gathered from the word of God from various versions of the Bible: the (NLT) New Living Translation Version, the (NIV) New International Version, (TLB) The Living Bible Version, the (NKJV) New King James Version, and the (KJV) King James Version. I thank God for granting me the wisdom and faith to write this message to be a blessing in someone life. God's grace and favor allowed me to write this book. He wrapped His arms around me and told me to go forward, and that is why I humbly take no credit for this creation. To God be the glory!

—Charlene Ward

CONTENTS

Introduction..xi

Chapter 1   God the Father.. 1

Chapter 2   God the Provider..18

Chapter 3   God the Protector...27

Chapter 4   God the Comforter 38

INTRODUCTION

This book is about the characteristics of God and what He represents. He is a Father, a Provider, a Protector, a Comforter and much more. He is God, and there is no other like Him. Consider yourself actually being wrapped in the Father's arms. Let's start with God's fingers. You can rest assure that with a touch of His fingertip we are protected and safe. We know that with His hands wide open, there are many blessings to receive from Him, which makes Him a provider. And when God wraps His arms around you, you are comforted with His love and kindness and mercy. He is considered the Father above all fathers for those who choose to believe and obey Him. He is the first person of the Godhead, known as the Father. He is the prime example of a father because He will protect you in time of trouble; He will make a way for you when all hope is gone, and He will comfort you in times of sorrow. Isn't that what a father should do for his children? He is the God of Abraham, Isaac, and Jacob. He is the God of yesterday, today, and forever more. Whatever you are going through, just pray this prayer of relief to Him ...

> Our Father which art in Heaven,
> Hallowed be thy name
> Thy kingdom come,
> Thy will be done in earth, as it is in heaven
> Give us this day our daily bread
> And forgive us our debts, as we forgive our debtors.
> And lead us not into temptations
> But deliver us from evil;
> For thou is the Kingdom, and the power, and the glory forever
> Amen.
> —Matthew 6:9 KJV

CHAPTER 1

GOD THE FATHER

What is a father? A father is defined as a male parent. There are many roles of a father. Traditionally, a father has been known as the head of the household. He is a person who is mostly respected, having absolute authority over his family. A father has the responsibility of protecting, supporting, and helping his family. A father is loving and caring. A father also disciplines his children when they are disobedient. He is the one who sets the rules of the household, which are supposed to be mirrored by the word of God.

There is a saying that any man can father a child, but it takes someone special to be a daddy. Although both are technically the same, one may argue that there is a difference between the two. In some cases, fathers have the inner responsibility to supply their families with the basic needs of clothing, shelter, and food. Dads, on the other hand, give guidance to their family as well as supply them with the basic necessities in life. The word *dad* is a term of affection and familiarity. Dads are more intimate and compassionate. Dad is someone who actively participates in a child's growth and development, both emotionally and spiritually. A father can be viewed in a natural or a spiritual sense. There are many individuals who can play the role of the father figure in one's life, but there can be only one daddy. And a dad can be a father of many children. A father in the natural sense is a daddy by statute and not by the title of his position. In this case, a father is more than someone who contributes to the physical creation of a child; he is more than a man from whom the sperm has been obtained to fertilize the mother's eggs. A dad finds satisfaction in interacting with his wife and children, and he is able to demonstrate more love to them than what a father can show. He is someone who has produced a child and is involved in the upbringing of that child. So we can conclude that the main difference between a father and a dad is that the father's relationship is merely biological while a dad's relationship is emotional. And the difference between the two is based on the child's view of his/her father or dad.

In the bible, the person known as Jehovah is God, and the Lord is the Son, known as Jesus Christ, who is the second part of the Godhead. Jesus works under the direction of the Father and is in complete harmony with Him. It is understood that all of humankind are brothers and sisters to Jesus, He being the eldest of the spirit children of God. Scripture says. "God created the heaven and the earth" (Genesis 1:1 KJV), or as Paul said, God created all things by Christ Jesus (Ephesians 3:9 KJV) because Jesus was at the beginning when the world was formed. (John 1:1 KJV) tells us that in the beginning was the Word, the Word was with God, and the Word was God. The Holy Ghost is also part of the Godhead and is variously called the Holy Spirit or the Spirit of God. Through the living and enduring word of God, we are born again, not from a natural seed, but of a supernatural seed. Just as a child starting to eat his or her own food, humankind must hunger for the true meat of the word and feed upon it. Mankind must eat the whole word and not leave any leftovers on the plate. When a child is wrapped in his or her father's arms, he or she feels a sense of security and safety. A spiritual father is one who contributes to the spiritual growth of a child as he steps in to be there in the absence of the biological father.

God is our ultimate Father. When one speaks of God, it is generally to the Father who is referred to as Elohim (powerful God). God the Father is omnipotent (all powerful), omniscient (all knowing), and omnipresent (everywhere). He is our heavenly Father. All humankind are His children. According to 2 Corinthians 6:17–18 (NIV), God tells us, "I will receive you, I will be a Father to you, and you will be my sons and daughters." And since we are sons and daughters of God, we should rightfully possess His Spirit. It is interesting how some parents allow their children to call them by their first name instead of calling them mom or dad. It is a question of respect. With God it is a matter of knowing Him and acknowledging who He is. Although God is reference by other names, there is still one God. We can not refer to Him as one of these idol Gods. That would be so disrespectful. We are not able to see Him, but God is able to show up and make Himself known at the right moment. When we feel alone, need protection, or are even in need of a financial blessing or spiritual uplifting, God will be by our side. We have to pray to Him and believe all things will work out for the good.

We are sons and daughters of God because of His love. In 1 John 3:1 (KJV), we are told, "Behold, what manner of love the Father hath bestowed upon us, that we should be called the sons of God: therefore the world knoweth us not, because it knew him not." We are a part of God's family. Because of His love, He has prepared a home for us in His kingdom to be treated as royalty. There is nothing wrong with showing love to your child. They need to hear the "I love you's" and receive the hugs and kisses from the father. There is hope that if we have the love abiding on the inside and show love to God we are able to show love to each other as He has shown to us. We will display the actions of the King's child, then we can see our Father one day.

THE SUBSTITUTE FATHER

God is a father to the fatherless. His love is so powerful and strong that He can be a father to so many people at the same time. Sometimes fathers are no longer around because of various circumstances. Some fathers leave their families by walking away from responsibilities, or they were never around at the beginning of their child's life in the first place. And unfortunately, some fathers may not be around because they leave by death. No matter what the reason may be, the mother is left to take care of her family. She is faced to be the mother and the father. She sometime desires the help of a male figure. She has to carefully choose the type of male role model that would be a positive influence in her children's lives, especially if she is raising a son. Even though it is often said that a woman does not need a man to validate her, it is in the male child's favor to have a father figure in his life—one who is encouraging and provides direction. Most of the time there is a grandfather or an uncle who steps up to the position. The father figure can introduce the male child to things that the mother is not capable of fully introducing to the child. The father figure is also needed for the upbringing of a girl. The father is able to teach the girl, through living example, how a man should properly treat a woman. The single mom is responsible for her children's well-being. If a mom decides to start over in a relationship after losing the father of her children, it is important that she understands the man she brings around her children considers her family to be a package deal. The love and attention from the man has to be genuine—and not just to please the mother. Rather, he must show love to the entire family. It is crucial that the man who enters a relationship with a woman with children is in the relationship with a sincere heart and doesn't just wish to be a temporary dad, because fatherhood is a full-time job. It is believed that when God places people in the lives of others, this is for a reason and purpose that no one should question and be cast away. Satan recognizes what is good, and it is his job to destroy and divide the good works of God. A family that is filled with love and divine structure is a good thing. Satan will try to destroy the good things God has put together, but only if you allow him.

The birth of a child should be felt as a blessing and not a burden. It is truly a gift when a child is brought into this world without any major problems. A woman has a difficult enough time laboring to bring a child into this world without worrying how she will take care of the child by herself. When the father is not present at the beginning of the child's life by his own choice, it can be so disappointing to the mother. She feels alone and abandoned, and that same feeling is sometimes absorbed by the child. The mother develops a sense of spitefulness and bitterness that becomes transparent. It is not good for the child to witness discord between a father and mother. A child growing up in a home of such disharmony, it creates an environment that leads the child to carry those same bitter feelings into his or her own home one day. The revolving cycle of dysfunctional behavior must be broken and remedied by the love of God. God is able to step in and not only wipe out the evil in the home, but He becomes a permanent resident of the home as long as He is welcomed. It has to first start in the place where the heart lies.

There are some parents who break up, but are willing to keep the relationship ongoing with the child. This is called co-parenting. Co-parenting is when one parent leaves the home, most of the time it is the father, and they come together to make the decisions as it relates to raising the child. They are willing to maintain the cohesiveness in the family for the sake of the child so the child will continue to experience the love from both parents. This is an unselfish sacrifice if the parents can make it work. In co-parenting family time and other activities are planned together, but the parents live in separate homes. It is an unconventional way to raise a child, but the love is shown.

At times, some children grow up having a stepfather. This is when the mom chooses to marry again and introduces her children to another father in the home. When one examines the historical meaning of the word *stepfather*, it can make one think that it is a step down or a step away from the biological father. This way of thinking brings about a negative connotation of the word *stepfather*, which does not have to be. Children begin to see the negative image of a stepfather, and as a result they can often begin treating the stepfather as an outsider. The stepfather then sees himself as not being a significant part of the family. He is cast aside and found to be less valued in the family. The stepfather becomes ostracized from the home, leaving him feeling like he does not count for anything. He feels that he is useless and that his presence does not matter. He starts to see his family, especially the children, viewing him in a different way. This is not of God. On a positive note, a stepfather can be looked upon as a step up from the biological father. He is stepping up and making the choice to be a part of an established family. This man is stepping in a role to help support the mom and the children to show love. Some children refer to the step dad not as a step father, but as an actual dad because he is considered as being a great example of a father.

Let's look at some examples of how a father influences the upbringing of a child. Picture this: A girl is reared in a family with a strong, hard-working father. The father loves his family and acts as a great supporter. The girl learns to cherish that father figure into her adult life. While she recalls the image of her father, she hopes to find a man with the same personification of her father for her future husband. She hopes to be a loving wife for a good man one day. Throughout her life she discovers that the man she cherished the most was not the great father she thought she knew. The father deceived his family. She learned that her father had flaws, which caused her to think twice about men. She develops a non-trusting relationship with every man she meets. She learn how to sabotage her relationships which drives men away. During her hurt and pain she turned to the one true father, which is her Father in heaven, for comfort. God says in Deuteronomy 31:6 (KJV), "Be strong and of good courage, fear not, nor be afraid of them: for the Lord thy God, he it is that doth go with thee; he will not fail thee, or forsake thee."

In another case, the great father figure is taken away from the family. The strong leader the daughter knew growing up now no longer exists. When a father abandons the home, the love the girl encountered from her childhood begins to fade away. The girl learns to survive with just the memory of her father. The girl is now a grown woman, and she starts to meet men who never measure up to the love of her father. She finds herself going from relationship to relationship in search of true love. While searching the bottom of the barrel, she sometimes does not make wise choices in men. After given up all hope, the woman discovers the love of God, who is now her Father through His Son Jesus Christ. She learns that God loves her so much that He gave His only begotten Son, Jesus Christ. So the only thing she has to do is surrender her life to Him. This is a prime example how God can be the Father to someone that they thought they never had; but in reality God is there the entire time. It is interesting that young girls cling to their fathers and hope for a husband who fits the image of their father. If only this was the same aspiration applied to the image of our heavenly Father. It is not always wise for a woman to choose a husband based on how she views her own father. What if her father is an abuser or an alcoholic? Will this be the type of man she will choose as a husband?

Then there is the son who grows up trying to mimic his father's behavior. He tries to be a respectful man like his father. He tries so hard to please his father and to be looked up by his own family. And what happens if the young man fails? He has no one to blame but himself because he is trying to emulate a person he could never be.

Growing up can be a pain when a father leaves his family while his son is young and needs his father the most. The son desires to form a relationship with his father, but the relationship becomes distant and even void. So who does the son turns to as a father figure? Who is there to fulfill that void of the role of a father in his life? In some cases, the young man will turn his life around to a 180-degree semicircle and land in the right direction. And in other circumstances, the young man will resort to other lifestyles as a substitute for not having that great dominant male in the family. The young man must obtain his own identity and find himself. When a son is abandoned by his father, it leaves that child not being able to identify who he is in life, or he finds it difficult to form a relationship with anyone else. For example, the male child grows up not being able to connect with other male role models because his father abandoned him. He becomes angry and builds an imaginary wall of hate toward people. At any rate, the experience of not having a father in the home can become a life-altering change for that son. The absence can impact a son's life from generation to generation. There becomes a scar that will never heal without the remedy of forgiveness found through the love of God.

Unfortunately, we don't get to choose our parents. Parents are just an instrument that the Lord uses to bring children into the world. There are traditional and nontraditional families. And there are some families who are loving and caring faith believers living under the power of God. The most important thing to know is, with God we do have a choice. We can choose to live for Him and walk in the path of righteousness, or we can live a sinful and destructive life and become bound for eternal damnation. At times God allows special people to enter our lives to replace the void of the absent father. It could be that devoted grandparent, an uncle, a close friend of the family, older brother, a teacher, or a pastor that helps in molding a person from a man into a real man. God is able to help a person learn the power of forgiveness and love once a person gives his or her life to Christ. This is the act of being born again. But how can a person be delivered from hurt by being born again? Nicodemus asked a question to Christ, which is found in John 3 (KJV): "How can a man be born again when he is old, can he enter the second time into his mother womb, and be born?" He was referring to a natural birth of humankind. Jesus let us know of a spiritual birth, which is by the cleansing of the soul through baptism. When humankind accepts Jesus as their Savior, then the first process of being born again has begun. Being wrapped in God's arms, you can rest to sure that He will take good care of us.

When a father leaves his child, there is a separation that cuts to the core of that child's soul. It leaves the child feeling displaced and searching for answers that can only be answered by the absent father or the heavenly Father. It is described as a physician performing major surgery. The surgeon begins cutting into the skin, separating part of your body. Then he removes the part that is damaged, causing you to feel incomplete. But God is the potter; we are the clay. We are the work of His hands (Isaiah 64:8 KJV). He is able to mend any broken life if it is ripped to pieces. Besides, God knows of everyone before the time of birth. He has a purpose and a plan for our lives, and it is up to each individual to play out his or her part that is intended. When you look carefully, it seems we are all on a stage playing some type of character while performing on this earth. The script is the Bible, and our director is God. We are seeking our applause, which is approval from our Father in heaven. If we perform our best, we will receive the greatest award, which is the crown of life. It will be presented on that great day of judgment. In all actuality, we are living in the real world, and it must be within our hearts, deep in our souls, to live the righteous life to walk this Christian journey.

The Bible tells us to honor our father and mother and our days will be prolonged. There are ten positive things to consider when it comes to your father: 1) Appreciate the fact that your father planted the seed that gave you birth. 2) Appreciate who your father is regardless of his flaws. 3) Appreciate how challenging the job of fatherhood can be and what some fathers give up for their children. 4) Appreciate your spiritual father who can teach you more at times than a natural father. 5) Tell and show your father how much you appreciate him. 6) Give your father a hug and a kiss, and smile at your father, especially on those days of struggles. 7) Tell your dad you love him every day. 8) Do something for your dad or with your dad. 9) Live life to the fullest and make your dad proud. 10) Thank God for each day your father is with you. What if your father is no longer with you, whether he passes away or just walks out of your life? What would you say to him if you could see him just one more time? There are so many things that one would have, could have, should have said or done while a person is living that they wait to say or do after they are gone.

An example of a father-child relationship should be described as the relationship between God and Jesus. Jesus Christ knew His role and where He stood with His Father. During His walk on earth, Jesus told others about His Father so that others can know Him as well.

He wanted the world to know about the greatness of His Father. He described His home in heaven as a wonderful kingdom, and we would be treated as royalty in His Father's kingdom. He let others know that in order to get to His Father, all must go through Him. This speaks of the love and closeness between the Father and Son. It is possible to have that same love and appreciation toward our natural father.

GOD'S DNA

When humankind comes to know God, really know God, they are expected to obtain God's DNA (deeper new anointing) through the Holy Spirit. According to Genesis 1:27 (KJV), "God created man in His own image." Therefore He is the Father of the universe. We possess two sets of DNA—one physical DNA from our earthly parents and one spiritual DNA from our heavenly Father, which is the Holy Spirit. In the natural, when a father produces a child, he expects his son or daughter to have some of his characteristics. This gives the father confirmation that the blood running through the child's veins is his blood. And it also makes the father very proud to call the child his own. When a parent produces a child, it gives the parent a sense of joy and pride watching that child grow up. The parent starts to make plans for the child's future, such as preparing for the child's education and career choice. It makes the parent feel they have done a great job contributing to their child's success.

Sometimes the paternity of the child is questioned. The father needs proof if he is the father of the child before he can bond with the child. Sometimes the outcome is good, and sometimes it is not so good. Nevertheless, the fate of the child's life is left unknown.

This is not the case with God. God will love us no matter who we are, for God knew us before we were in our mother's womb (Jeremiah 1:5

KJV). God knows all about us. God the Father created the universe and everything in it. He is a big God, but at the same time He is a personal God who knows each person's every need. Jesus said God knows us so well He knows the number of hairs on each person's head. He knows our hearts, and He knows our thoughts and our ways. He knows our destiny and our future. His plan for us is to fulfill our destiny, so we must walk therein. It does not matter about our geographic location, our pedigree, or our financial status. God wants us to live according to His way, but He cannot tolerate our sins. Through the confession of our sins, He will claim us as His children. It is God's intent that man walks and acts as He does. We do not need a birth certificate or a blood test to know who God is in our lives. Man is literally God's offspring, made in His image, whereas all other things are but the work of His hands (Acts 17:28–29 KJV). It pleases God to know that man is willing to follow Him and obey His word. When humans make the choice to do the opposite of God's command and go their own way, this action disappoints the Father. People can possess the same qualities and spirituality of God through His Son, Jesus Christ. A deeper new anointing is a new walk with God, which can be acquired through the Holy Spirit.

John 3:6 (NLT) says, "Humans can reproduce only human life, but the Holy Spirit gives new life from heaven." When we received the gift of eternal life through our acceptance of Jesus Christ as our Lord and Savior, God breathed new life into us, bringing a spiritual birth. At that moment we received heavenly DNA into our souls in the form of the Holy Spirit.

God allowed Mary to conceive a child (baby Jesus) without having intercourse. There was no form of modern-day scientific conception, known today as artificial insemination. Mary was the carrier, but God was the maker of this seed fertilized by the Holy Spirit. This was the only time that blood was not transmitted from one blood line to the other. For this reason, Christ's conception and birth was known to be a supernatural birth, the greatest miracle of this world. He was born in the lowest condition, in a stable, and placed in a manger, which was something that an animal was fed out of. Christ's mother accepted her calling and was obedient to God's plan. And Christ inherited the Holy Spirit while in His mother's womb. He was blessed as the rightful heir to the heavenly throne as the Son of God.

So we see that Jesus carries the same DNA as His Father God through the Holy Spirit. Jesus was destined and ordained to be the example of the true and living God. He is the second being that makes the framework of the Godhead. It is impossible to accept one without acknowledging the other. John 10:30 (KJV), says "I and my Father are one."

With God's DNA inside of us, the divine life of the Holy Spirit grows within us. Now we are different than the rest of the world. We are part of a distinct race. We are known to be a chosen generation, a royal priesthood, a holy nation, a peculiar people walking upright, knowing that we are kings and queens related to the living God. We resemble our heavenly Father as evidenced by our new Christ-like attitudes, motivations, perspectives, desires, goals, and godly value system. Christians have a deep desire to be a blessing to others as God has been a blessing to us. After our spiritual births, we are connected eternally to God in such a way that even when we fall, our heavenly genetic link to Him will not be broken because of the power of repentance.

When humankind learns to search their hearts, they will see Jesus Christ living deep within. With all of His glory, they will realize that the best desire is to glorify the Father, the one who sent Him, and most of all, not to let His glory be diminished. He deserves the complete glory that men can and must give to their Father and Maker, and still more as the Author of their redemption!

Because of God giving us a Savior—Jesus Christ, our brother who advocates for our behalf—we are able to dust off our sins and prove ourselves worthy of being called one of His children. A real parent never gives up on his or her child. The child may go astray and do things in the world, but the parent always stay connected with the child, either through prayer or thoughts until the end of time. Even on the cross, Jesus Christ knew He was connected with the Father. He was willing to accept His death, knowing He would be with the One who created Him. "Then Jesus, calling out with a loud voice, said, 'Father, into your hands I commit my spirit!' And having said this he breathed his last" (Luke 23:46 NKJV). This was a true act of undisputed love between a Father and His Son.

DISCIPLINARIAN IN ACTION

In many cultures, you find the father making the decisions and setting the tone of the family. The tone can be heard through learning of God's word. The father must demonstrate that he is a positive motivating force in the life of his children. His disciplinary action will need to be shown in a way to build up a child, not tear the child down. The role of a father is so crucial in a child's life because he brings order within the upbringing of a child's life. Through discipline and understanding, the child can learn structure and much respect for his parents as well as others in an authoritative position. It is up to the father to regulate the home in a manner that the child will live a productive life. It is obvious that the presence of a father can leave a lasting impression on a child's life.

During a little girl's childhood, a father can make his daughter feel as though she is the most special thing in the world. The father cherishes his daughter, and he tries to give her any and every thing that she wants. No other man will love a girl the way a father loves his daughter. The father's role is to make his daughter feel special but not spoiled to the point that no other man will be able to please her. This will become a problem in her adult life. The girl begins to think no man is good enough for her because her father has ruined her for any other man to provide for her. The daughter becomes dependent on her father and finds it difficult to allow anyone to provide for her or even provide for herself. It's fine to treat your child special sometimes. There is a big difference between treating someone special and spoiling him or her. A spoiled child looks for something all the time and has a "me-first" attitude. These children whine, pout, and throw tantrums to have their way. The Bible tells us that if you spare the rod you will spoil the child. If you spare the rod, you can end up with a child that does not accept the word *no*. The rod represents discipline and sometimes can be used as a lesson learned or a lesson burned. There are some parents who find it difficult to follow this value. They find it hard to say no to their children, especially to little girls. It is okay to show love to your child, but it is also okay to set boundaries by abstaining from giving your child everything. Children who get everything may grow up thinking that the world owes them, and they feel a sense of entitlement. Their ways and attitudes may cause them to face things in this world that the father is not able to fix.

It is important for a father to teach his child right from wrong and practice what he preaches. The philosophy of "doing as I say and not as I do" can lead a child to be confused and into trouble. It is a good thing for a father to show his children that serving the Lord is the way. The Bible teaches us certain laws in life, such as those found in the Ten Commandments and throughout the teachings of Jesus Christ. Christ teaches us how we should have the right attitude of life found in Matthew 5:3–11, called the *B* attitude. A father can be that real-life example to demonstrate how to be a servant of the Lord. The example that a father shows in a child's life can determine a guilty or not-guilty verdict for a life sentence for his child. It can mean the difference between a child living a successful or unsuccessful life for the rest of his or her future.

As indicated in Deuteronomy 28, believe it or not the sins of the father are an unforgettable event. When people commit a sin and think they will get away with it, it comes back later in life. It may even show up in the child's life one day because he or she has witnessed the life of the father's sin. The child will sometimes imitate the behavior. There is an old saying, "If a child disrespects his or her parent, and when he or she have children, his or her child will treat him or her the same way he or she treated his or her parent." If this is the case, then the world of parenting is like a domino effect. One behavior knocks down another, then another, and then another until nothing is left standing long enough to learn a valuable lesson. It becomes a world filled with terrible people with "bad" behaviors. And the word lets us know that people are responsible for their own sins. Psalm 20:11 (KJV) tells us, "Even a child is known by his doings whether his work be pure, and whether it be right." The world uses "time-out" to teach a child consequences when the child misbehaves or does something wrong. The father can take the time out to teach the child God's word, and the child might grow up appreciating and respecting the law of the land much better. The Bible tells us in Proverbs 22 to train up a child in a way he should go and when he gets older he will not depart from his teachings.

The most painful punishment is when you are punished by God. No one should want to face the wrath of an angry God for being disobedient. Look at what happened to Adam and Eve when they disobeyed God when they ate the forbidden fruit. Humankind was never the same, and the world became a less peaceful place to live. God allowed Adam and Eve to live, but they learned a vital lesson about obedience. And although Moses led the children to the land of Canaan, he did not live to see the Promised Land because of his disobedience.

When God punishes you, it is a lesson you will never forget. You will either straighten up or head for destruction. Have you knowingly done something wrong and you had to go to your parents and own up to your wrongdoing? You don't know what may happen or what they might say. You hesitate to have that conversation, but when you finally get the guts to do so, you fear the worst. Even though you have disappointed your parents, you are relieved that you got it all out. So, imagine how God feels when you disappoint Him time after time, being disobedient and sinning again and again. He is our Father, and He wants us to own up to our sin, repent, and do right. And even though He forgives us, there is still a limit and consequences for our sinful behavior. One thing about it, when we disappoint God He lets us know, and then He issues the consequence, which is a lesson learned. But we have to want to make it right.

CHAPTER 2

GOD THE PROVIDER

Fathers are often regarded as merely breadwinners who fulfill their paternal duties by providing for their families. A father is there for his children until they are able to take care of themselves, and even after the child is all grown up, the father will see about his children in times of need. The man who is always there for his children is a true daddy, one who shows responsibility and stability for his children. Men who lack the responsibility and courage to support and provide for their children are considered deadbeat dads. Have you wonder about the word *deadbeat*

and what it really means? When we look at the word *dead*, it means having lost life, no longer alive. It also means no longer in existence, no longer having significance or relevance. The word *beat* in urban terms means a lame situation or to take something from someone. The modern dictionary gives a definition meaning to hurt, injure, to cause pain. A deadbeat dad or father is a father who neglects his responsibilities as a parent—a father who does not provide for his children that he had a part in creating. He is a father who does not have morals enough to realize how difficult he is making life for his family and causing his family grief. It is the same grief as if someone dies. A deadbeat dad is someone who lacks feelings or is not sensitive to the needs of his family, therefore causing pain and hurt. He leaves his family to struggle feeling beaten and bruised financially and emotionally. The deadbeat dad wants to appear that he can be a responsible dad just because he fathered a baby. But when it's time to pay the bills and actually take care of his child, he is not able to supply. He is sometimes made to take care of his child through the court system. He stands before a man in a robe, in judgment determining whether is he is a responsible person. But why should it take these drastic steps? The deadbeat dad has to prove that he provides for his child or give excuses as to why he can't provide for his child. Nevertheless, it is an uncomfortable situation that makes the dad appears negligent and irresponsible. The dad is made to feel less than a person because he fathered a child and does not take care of the child. He is able to reproduce but does not produce the goods or the means to take care of his child that he claims he loves. He comes up with every reason, whether it is true or not true, for why he does not support his child. He becomes an occasional father, one who finds a way to give on special occasions—for instance birthdays and Christmas. The occasional father believes he is doing his part in providing for his child, but in actuality, it's the father's responsibility to take care of his baby. When a seed is planted, it requires nurturing, feeding, love and monitoring for it to grow. It is the same when a man chooses to lay down with a woman and plant his seed and then produces a child. His decision to lay with other women and produce other children has become as easy as sitting on the couch and turning on the television to watch it, not knowing what might come on next. Personally speaking, if the dad would lift the same finger that he used to turn on the television and get a job, he would become a provider for his child, who needs him all year round.

During the times of the pioneers, the father was the one who went out to gather food for his family. He hunted or farmed to provide for his family. The father did not hesitate to do all he knew to support his family. It was the very strength of the father's dominant character that let the family know he could be dependable, reliable, and supportive. When fathers left the home, it was to provide for their families, such as to find work. And the dedicated father always returned home. But when times got tough and the father had to leave his family, sometimes there was no guarantee that the father would return. What does the family do in this case? The family must take on the teachings and example left by the father. This is one of the reasons a good father is respected in a household and the family follows his lead.

Man has grown weaker in his responsibility of being the ultimate provider. Many may agree that the government has had some influence in stripping fathers from their role as providers. Government assistance (welfare), as we know, became the enabling system that drove many men to slack off from their ability to financially support their families. In some sense, welfare took the place of the father in the home. Mothers could wait until the first of the month (check day) to buy food for the family. Government assistance, such as food stamps, became the breadwinner. The mom would look forward to going to the store during certain times of the month and proudly load up her shopping cart with groceries purchased by her food stamps card. So why should the dad go out to support his family when they were being fed and clothed by other means? And with the rent paid through housing assistance, they had a place to live. In retrospect, government assistance has helped some families get on their feet, and they chose to get off welfare. This was the design of welfare, to be a temporary assistance, not long term. Many people have latched on the idea of taking advantage of the government and allowing the government to pay them back for the suffering and hardship that was endured from the past. But whatever happened to the concept of working to get paid? It has become backwards nowadays. Some people want to get paid without work. You have to put something in to get something in return.

Our heavenly Father is our most gracious provider. God will pay us for the work we do and the work we don't do. God is not dead; He is much alive. God is known as *Jehovah Jireh*, our Provider (Genesis 22:14). The Bible tells us that the Lord will provide. He will fill the void of the absent dad and supply all our needs. Paul tells us in Philippians 4:19 about the promise of God—that He will provide all of our needs according to His riches in glory in Christ Jesus. God is our shepherd, and we shall not want for anything in this world. "For the earth is the Lord and the fullness thereof, the world, and they that dwell therein" (Psalm 24:1KJV). Therefore, everything belongs to God because He made the earth and He is able to supply us with the things from the earth. God knows the very thing we have need of. Just read Matthew 14:13–21. It is a prime example that God will provide. Jesus fed five thousand with just five loaves of bread and two fish. Now you may wonder how it was possible. It was by the power that was given to Him from His heavenly Father. Ephesians 3:20 (NIV) words it best: "Now to him who is able to do immeasurably more than all we ask or imagine, according to his power that is at work within us." The food kept coming and coming until the multitude of people were fed. We can follow the instructions found in Matthew 6:33 (KJV), "Seek ye first the kingdom of God, and his righteousness; and all these things shall be added unto you." The lesson learned is that we should not worry about the things of this world because whatever we need, God has it.

God will show favor to those who put their trust in Him. The greatest gift that God gave to humankind is the gift of salvation through His Son, Jesus Christ. John 3:16 (KJV) says "For God so loved the world, that He gave His only begotten Son, that whosoever believes in Him shall not perish, but have eternal life." The kingdom of heaven is the most priceless gift there is. It is a home not of this world, filled with many mansions. In order to possess the keys to this heavenly home, one must be saved. In my Father's kingdom you will not have a want or need for anything. The land is filled of abundance and plenty of love. In God's land, you would want for nothing. In the kingdom of heaven, there is no heartache, pain, sickness, or sorrow. Can you just imagine? Every day will be like Sunday, rejoicing and singing songs of praise unto our Lord. Who wouldn't want to receive a wonderful gift like this from God? A mansion, your own home that will not foreclose, and you will never have to worry about payments because our Father has taken care of that for us. You won't have to worry about the lights ever getting turned off, because they will always be lit. You won't have to worry about repairs because the structure will be built on a solid foundation.

THE INHERITANCE OF GOD

Fathers should establish an inheritance that places an everlasting financial reward for their children. It should be in a form of a will or legal document that is honored by the courts. Proverbs 13:22 (KJV) says, "A good man leaves an inheritance to his children's children: and the wealth of the sinner is laid up for the just." It is within a father's best interest to leave something good as a reminder or legacy for his children to remember him after he passes away. Whether it's words of wisdom or an item to cherish, this is called the blessings of the father.

It starts in the delivery room. After waiting nine months for the birth of a child to come out of the mother's womb the doctor says, "It's a boy" or "It's a girl." The parents are excited about the new bundle of joy entering into their lives. The parents start to make plans for their child's life with much enthusiasm. They put money aside for their child's future. This same joy parents display is compared to God's joy when we are born again into a spiritual birth. Remember the story when Jesus Christ was baptized by John the Baptist. As soon as Jesus was baptized, He came up out of the water. At that moment heaven was opened, and He saw the spirit of God descending like a dove and a light fell on Him. A voice from heaven said, "This is my son, whom I love; with him I am well pleased." It pleases our Father to see His child enter into a spiritual world, a new birth filled with righteousness and cleansed from sin. Jesus, the Son of God, went through four miraculous phases on this earth: His birth, His life, His death, and His resurrection. He did so with humility because it was His Father's plan.

A father sets the tone of being a giver. He gives love, peace, happiness, support, and financial stability. When the family sees that the father is a giver, they are inspired to have the same qualities. If a father, being evil, know how to give good gifts to his children, how much more will the Father who is in heaven give good things to those who ask Him? And when you give; be a cheerful giver and make sure it is rightfully gained. Because God the Father is concerned about His children's well-being, He gives to the just and even allows the unjust to prosper. That's just the kind of Father He is. God is the greatest giver of them all.

A father will have to demonstrate that he is not only a giver but an honest one. "It is a wonderful heritage to have an honest father" (Proverbs 20:7 TLB). When a father is not a giver, especially to his family, he is demonstrating a selfish act. A father with integrity works hard to be that great provider. He sometimes takes on two or three jobs to make sure his family has a decent life. When a father leaves his family stranded, he is considering his own needs rather than his family's needs. Eventually the things the father does come back to haunt him. It is called reaping what you sowed. It is so simple. If you sow good seed, you will reap good things. When you give, it will be given unto you, pressed down, running over, and in good measure.

God is the wealthiest giver of all time when it comes to giving gifts. He gives us the desires of our hearts, and He knows just what we need before we ask of Him. He has left us with a spiritual insurance policy that contains treasures that cannot be kept in this earthly vessel. This insurance policy is the Holy Bible, which consists of great instructions about the way man must live in order to inherit the keys to the kingdom of heaven. The word *insurance* assures us that with God we cannot fail, with God we can do anything, with God we can make it, and without God we are nothing. With any insurance policy you will find a designated beneficiary. The best thing about it is that God has many beneficiaries assigned to His insurance policy. You need to ask yourself if you want to be one of His beneficiaries. When we learn to tap into the treasures, which are the blessings from God, we can experience His purpose and plan for our lives through His powerful glory. We can learn of His will. It is not His intention that we should fall short of His many blessings. The woman described in the parable in Luke 15:8–10 thought she had swept her silver coin away. You may asked, why didn't she light a lamp and sweep the entire house and search carefully until she finds it? When she finds it, she will call her friends and neighbors to rejoice with her. When God does something for us, it is worth rejoicing over and giving Him the praise because it is the will of God that allows us to have the things on this earth as well as in heaven. "Whatever is bind on earth will be bound in heaven and whatever is loose on earth is loosed in heaven" (Matthew 18:18 KJV). Romans 4:17 (KJV) tells us that we must "call those things which be not as though they were." The scripture can have many interpretations as it applies to one's circumstance, but in this case it means that God can elevate you into greater things, greater positions, and greater wealth if you only speak it into existence as if it has already happened. You have to count the situation already done in your mind and in your heart.

As stated before, we can find the many blessings from our Father throughout the Bible. We see that the bloodline is originated through the seed of the father. In the Old Testament, God blessed Abraham, who blessed Isaac; Isaac blessed Jacob; Jacob blessed his twelve sons. God blessed Abraham with a son during his old age. He told Abraham that he would be blessed and his seed would be blessed. Our Father's strategic plan is to bless His children if we are first obedient and faithful to His instructions. Galatians 3:29 (KJV) tell us, "If ye be Christ's, then are ye Abraham's seed, and heirs according to the promise." This means that God's promise is not broken starting with Abraham, from generation to generation. He blesses those who trust Him and believe in His Son, Jesus Christ, from now until the end of time. God's blessings are beyond measure. His blessings are amazing and very gratifying. His blessings are greater than the fortune of this world. When people receive rewards from the world, people have a tendency to spend more than their fair share. When God blesses you, He gives you the things you need, which are more than enough, and it is right on time.

It is common for the saints of God to be tempted with the materialistic things of this world. Most people look at the things they want instead of the things they need. God will supply all our needs according to His riches and glory by Christ Jesus. God will not withhold any good thing from His children. God does not want His children to be without anything. In the sight of God we find that charity and love work hand in hand. So if we learn to obtain a spiritual mind-set, man will learn that it is acceptable to give. Humankind should love giving from the heart and not out of greed or lust.

If we strive to take out the lust of this world and apply the word of God then we can see ourselves richly prospering. Just look closely at the word *world*. When you take the letter l out, you will have the word. If you look at 1 John 2:16 (KJV), it tells us, "For all that is in the world, the lust of the flesh, and the lust of the eyes, and the pride of life, is not of the Father, but is of the world." God wants us to have the things of the world, but we must not forget how the things are provided to us, and we must not allow the things of this world to overcome our thoughts and hearts with greed. In time of hardship, we need the word to carry us through.

No matter how big or small the need, God will provide. His blessings are guaranteed, and you can count on Him doing just what He says. It is like taking money to the bank; you are certain you will be able to withdraw from your account when you need it. Therefore, when you need God to do something in your life, you have to know and trust He will be there to make it happen. Can you think of any time that God has made a way out of no way in your life? It makes it hard to explain how you came out of the circumstance, doesn't it? Well, His works are unseen, not like humans, and His ways are not like humans' ways. He has all power to do anything, everything, anywhere, at any time, but it takes non-doubting faith. Faith is the key that unlocks the door to any situation. If you have faith in God's ability to do, then you will see the results of His works. Because according to Hebrews 11:1 (KJV), "Faith is the substance of the things hope for, the evidence of things not seen." So the evidence of your situation or problem has already been worked out because of your faith. And for those people who think things work out because of their own doings, they are mistaken. This may be the case for non-believers. Think on this: God is so merciful that He allows things to happen even when we don't believe He is involved. Some may not acknowledge God's involvement in situations that turn out good, but they are acknowledged by Him. Remember, He has all power.

CHAPTER 3

GOD THE PROTECTOR

A house is symbolic of a family. The father is the foundation. Even though you may disagree and say that God is the foundation, just open your mind to this conclusion. The reason the father is considered the foundation is that everything built sits on the father's standards. It can be weak or strong. Hopefully the standard or blueprint is constructed through the word of God. When the father learns to arm himself with the armor of God and to protect himself with the truth and have the breastplate of righteousness, while keeping his feet resting on the gospel of peace and taking on the shield of faith and wearing the helmet of salvation as he maintains the sword of the Spirit, which is the word of

God, then he is able to stand strong, and he can fight against anything that will be a threat to his foundation as written in Ephesians 6:10–18.

The side structure of the house is a good mother placed by the father's side, supporting him. Everything else in the house is the family, which is placed in the house supported by the foundation of the father. If the foundation gives away then everything else is destroyed. The house must also have a roof to protect the family from the storm and rain. This roof represents God's covenant with the family. You see, there is a purpose as to why the roof is placed on top of the house. God should be at the top over our lives and not at the bottom. In most historically designed houses, the rooftops are made in a triangular shape. Picture the design as the shape of the divine holy trinity, representing the Father, the Son, and the Holy Spirit. God's love and covenant will not allow the family's house to crumble unless man becomes disobedient and strays away from Him. When there is a crack in the foundation, such as a troubled father, the house begins to deteriorate and needs to be restored. The windows begin to break, and the roof starts to leak. There is nothing worse than a house divided and torn down. For this reason, it is important that the father has a close relationship with God to maintain the balance of the home. If the house does fall, God can restore all that has fallen. It will take much prayer and strong faith to bring the family back together again. Building your house on a solid foundation takes being connected with God. If you lose your connection with Him, it is impossible for Him to operate in your life. Look at the way you use your cell phone. It operates through a transmitter signaling from your phone to a tower. Somehow it has to be connected through the carrier of that tower. If there is no tower in the area, then you have no service or a weak signal. When you talk on the phone, the message bounces from the tower and transfers to the person's phone on the other end of the receiver so he or she is able to hear you. The message goes back and forth as the conversation continues. This process is more technical than explained, but the short version was provided. So imagine this method working in the spiritual realm. God the Father is that tower, and Christ is the transmitter sending our message to the Father. We communicate by praying to Christ, and he sends the message to God. This is the connection we have with God, and with Him we will always have the service made available to us.

Although the father is known as the protector and the strength of the family, the mom is the lioness of the family when her family is faced with adversity. The Bible tells us that women must submit themselves to their husbands as to the Lord. *Submit* is a humble word, and it takes strength to do so. Being submissive shows the pure, reverent, and yet gentle and quiet spirit that is precious to God. It is observed and admired by others around you, overlooking the fancy hairdos, lavish clothes, and shining jewelry that is being worn. But what does the word *submit* really means? According to *Roget's II Thesaurus*, the definition of submit is to give in, to commit to the consideration or judgment of another, and to turn in, such as a paper or project. There are many command words involved in the definition: "give in, commit, and turn in." They all have one thing in common: surrender. And this is the meaning that most people see when they look at the verse regarding wives submitting to their husbands. But, what happens when a woman submits and her husband leaves her and she is left to support herself? She has to learn to stand strong and operate on the offensive instead of being helpless. The woman has been taught all her life that the man is to be head, the leader of the home, and then he ups and leaves the home. The woman is then forced to stand on her own to support her family. She has to go out and get a job and use her instincts to provide for her family. The humbleness has now vanished, and she has become a survivor and an authority figure. Now this scenario is not meant to prove the Bible wrong about women being submissive. It is to explain the position that women are subject to be courageous when faced with a challenge. Women should be taught to walk beside the man rather than behind or below the man. Wasn't it God who made woman from the side of man? She was not made from the man's feet or his head; it was his side. And it was a great thing because God could have made her the same way He made man, from dust. He wanted woman to be a part of man to walk with man and be by his side; not ahead or below or in front or behind, but beside. That's why the word *submit* is so controversial in the Bible. It sparks up many conversations in the church and during family gatherings. You will have to research it for yourself and gather your own understanding.

In the animal world, the male animal fights off anything that poses a threat to his family. He protects his family to the depth of his being. And even though the male animal may be defeated, he still carries the image of superiority to his family. The same is viewed within the human species. At times the mother is forced to be dominant, yet her domineering spirit is portrayed as being disrespectful and rude because society does not expect the mother to be the outspoken party in the family. The father being superior and not inferior causes the rest of the family to honor and respect his authority. He represents the lion king of the family, and he will do what it takes to defend his family. But when there is a weak father in the home, then the enemy is subject to go in and take over the family. It's hard for a father to sit back while his child is struggling. The father becomes helpless. He comes to the realization that he is only a man, and it is beyond his control. He has to learn to give the problem to something bigger and mightier than he.

Just as a natural father protects his children, God is a protector to His children as well. Jehovah-Sabaoth means *the Lord Host our Protector* (Psalm 46:7), Jehovah-Magen means *the Lord the Shield* (Deut. 33:29), and Jehovah-Machsi means the *Lord my Refuge* (Psalm 91:9). God's love for His children allows us to have the power to defend against the wiles of the enemy. He is our shield of protection. We can rest assured that if we put on the whole armor of God through His holy word, He will fight our battles for us. When all our fight is gone, He lets us know that the battle is not ours; it belongs to the Lord. There are a number of metaphors referring to God's protection for His people. He is our Shield, Fortress, Hiding Place, Keeper, Rock, Shade, Shelter, Stronghold, and Refuge. According to Psalm 9:1–2 (KJV), "He that dwelleth in the secret place of the most High shall abide under the shadow of the Almighty. He is my refuge and my fortress: my God: in him will I trust." In times of trouble and in times of need, the Lord will protect us and shield us from all hurt, harm, and danger. He sees trouble ahead, and He will cause you to go another route. Just as a detour sign directs you to another route, God will lead you another way so you will not enter troubled waters. We must trust and obey Him enough to do what He tells us. The mistake that man makes is that he tries to do things on his own. He wants us to write our visions and make it plan and trust Him to see it through.

The Lord God is our rock, a rock of strength and courage. That rock does not crumble or crack when times get tough. Sometimes God allows us to go through things so we can recognize His glory. And He is walking with us every step of the way. His hands are strong enough and mighty enough to carry us through difficult times. And God is so concerned about His children that He places us in a safe place after we have gone through the storm in life. He is so great and awesome, which makes Him the greatest Daddy of them all.

THE HERO

In most daughters' eyes a father is her hero in the family. The father has a special relationship with his daughter that allows him to protect her when she is going through a difficult time. The father makes his family feels safe and secure. We find that most homes have a security system installed, as well as many business and vehicles. It makes the owner feels secure and confidence that their property is protected. There is a sense of trust that if anyone or anything attempts to invade on the property, the alarm will activate and make the owners aware that they are being violated and there is an intruder.

Having a secure relationship with God provides us with a trustworthy fulfillment that lets us know we are protected under the blood of His Son, Jesus Christ. A relationship is mostly defined as an emotional, spiritual, or physical connection with someone. Although we think we are protected by an alarm system installed by a company, it is God who actually sends into the heart of man to avoid going to your home, your vehicle, and your business. And even if at times it is allowed, then we can still say, "Thank You, Lord," for protecting lives and for being able to recover the things that were lost or damaged. Besides, they are only materialistic things that can be restored. When you are secure in God, there is a connection to His holy system. When the enemy attempts to violate your soul and disturbs your property of peace, the alarm, which is the Holy Spirit, goes off to alert you. Sometimes we don't always see ahead on the road. God speaks to us to let us know we need to go another way because there is danger ahead. We must obey His voice because He knows all things.

A father is known to provide for his family, and he saves the day. For this reason, he is looked at as a hero. He gives his child money for ice cream or to go shopping. He is looked as getting the needs met for the family. A father should secure his home and make sure all members of the family are home before he lays his head on the pillow. When a father feels that his family is in danger, he acts on the behalf of his family to rescue them. No true father wants to see his child hurt. Imagine a girl going to her father in distress and emotionally hurt. The father immediately notices his daughter crying, and he assumes that somebody has done something to her. He starts to question what or who caused her harm, but in all actuality, the daughter was in a car accident and she went to her father to tell him what happened. You can see how the father's protective alarm is raised to shield his daughter from hurt, harm, or danger. It is the same radar that goes off when a father has to protect his child through the true living word. He teaches his children that it is not the material weapon that the world is equipped with but the weapon of the Lord. Actually, a father rooted and grounded in the word of God leads and instructs his children to use the covenant of God as a shield and the word of God as a sword. He lets his children know that "no weapon form against thee shall prosper." The word of God teaches us that God will fight our battles. He lets us know that we cannot fight physically as the world fights, but we must fight a spiritual fight, on our knees by praying.

When you look at it, the world has a way of letting you know that the enemy exists. The enemy is portrayed in the movies, books, and even comics or cartoons as a villain. Batman had the Joker, the Riddler, and the Penguin. Superman had Lex Luther, and even when you look at the road runner, there was the coyote who always plotted to destroy the fast bird. Although these are fictional characters, the enemy does exists.

In life we may go to war with the enemy, but God is the Commander in charge that steers us and drives us to defeat the enemy. Whatever problem we face, God is there to protect us and keep us from harm's way. We may not always see the enemy coming, but God prepares us with the discerning of the Holy Spirit. Ephesians 6:12 (TLB) says: "For we are not fighting against people made of flesh and blood, but against persons without bodies-the evil rulers of the unseen world, those mighty satanic beings and great evil princes of darkness who rule this world; and against huge numbers of wicked spirits in the spirit world." There are things in this world that may try to bring us down—competition, finances, jealousy, and sometimes just our own faulty thinking. A lot of times our fight is within ourselves. We think people are saying bad things about us. The enemy puts negative things in our minds to distort and distract our thoughts of good. We need to concentrate on the goodness of our Lord and all He has done and is able to do for us. It is important to surround yourself with positive people and influences to guide you in the right directions. Pick and choose your role model and your hero carefully.

When there is a crisis in the family, people normally turn to the father for answers. The father has to maintain his integrity and cool because he knows that his family is counting on him. He cannot allow his family to see him weaken because they will then see the vulnerable side of him. There is one thing to learn from being weakened: the faith of God has to be bigger than your fears. We all grow weary and worry about things not working out. The strength of God that rests in us will soon come out, and we will prevail. It takes confidence and not fear nestled in your mind and heart because confidence and fear do not mix. Second Timothy 1:7 (NLT) says "God has not given us the spirit of timidness (fear) but of power, love and of self-control (sound mind)." We cannot allow fear to overtake our lives. Living in fear and with fear can allow us to miss our blessings. We have to pack the bag of fear and put it out of our lives for good because the Lord is our Shepherd, and even though we may sometimes walk through darkness, we must not fear the evil that surrounds us. If you have the courage to conquer your fears, then the Hero lives in you.

Everybody loves a hero. So what is a hero? A hero is a person who possesses heroic qualities or has performed a heroic act and is regarded as a model person. A hero is mostly a person of distinguished courage or ability, admired for his deeds and nobleness. Just as a superhero changes from a mortal to a greater being, we also go through an inner metamorphosis that causes us to think and believe we can do great things with the help of the Lord. It takes that supernatural faith to believe we can make it through the hard times and through the sad times in life. It's time to acknowledge the hero in our lives. We can pray and study God's word to help us. We wait on Him to give us the strength to pick us up and turn the situation around. When we were drowning deep in sin and we needed to be rescued by a life preserver, God stepped in and provided that life jacket and wrapped us up into salvation. We were made whole again and made to feel victorious. Now we can feel like a superhero and feel we can make it through any obstacles that come our way. No matter how big the mountain, we can speak to that mountain and command it to move.

When a soldier returns home from war, he is known as a hero. He receives the honor and recognition of someone who has survived in a war. He sometimes receives a medal to remind him who he is and what he means to his country. With God, we don't need a medal because we are warriors and soldiers of the King's army. We fight every day to resist sin and tell others about the goodness of Christ. We are ambassadors of the Lord working toward His kingdom. And when we get to heaven, we will receive our reward our medal of honor. But the greatest honor is hearing the Lord say, "Well done good and faithful servant: thou hast been faithful over a few things, I will make you ruler over many things: enter thou into the joy of thy Lord" (Matthew 25:21 KJV).

When people grow weak in their faith, they look for someone to rescue them, like a superhero swooping down to save them. The faith and belief in the Lord's promise that He will always be there for us is enough to know that we have a hero in the Lord. If you could picture the Lord wearing an S on His chest, it would stand for "Savior," but He does not need it. The Lord is able to stand strong on His promises. He is God all by Himself, and He does not need any help. Even when Satan tempted His Son, Jesus, three times, Jesus did not give in or give up. He knew and had faith in the God He served. He trusted His heavenly Father to be His shield and protector. He knew that everything He had was given to Him by His heavenly Father, and He did not worry. This is the kind of faith we all must have in order to carry us through. Through conception, we know that the natural father is responsible for giving us life, but we also need the heavenly Father to give us eternal life through Jesus Christ. Jesus is our hero in times of trouble. Jesus is there all the time, especially when the natural father is not there. He takes away the burden and helps a man to transition from just being a man to becoming a real man.

From the time a man is born, he is faced with the expectation that he must succeed in life. He starts out as a small, innocent baby and then develops into a great male with the survival skills to accomplish many things in this world. As a baby he must first learn how to turn over, then crawl and walk. Then he must learn how to say a few words that make sense. Then he must learn how to feed himself and use the bathroom. Later in life he must learn how to dress himself and start school to learn how to read and write in hopes to one day get a decent job. This great expectation given to man was first established when God made man to rule the land and everything in it. Man, referred to as Adam, was charged to attend to the animals and named them one by one. He was expected to live in peace and not want for anything in this special paradise called Eden. Man was the master of his own paradise because he was one of his kind, made after the image of God. All the animals and little creatures looked up to Adam, and he related to them well. The most heroic thing Adam did was being obedient to God and communing with God in the garden of Eden. God was pleased seeing Adam in the Garden. He was not to go outside the garden or he would lose his connection to God. But with the help of woman, man allowed himself to be deceived by the enemy, and he disobeyed God.

Here is the point: when you count on someone being there and doing what he or she is supposed to do, it makes you feel like that person can do no wrong. But when that person disappoints you and you see the person has the ability to fail, then you find it hard to rely on that person again. No one wants to be in a place where they are let down, disappointed. It is a hurtful feeling, a feeling of non-trust. When some people find themselves about to feel the feeling of non-trust, they have a tendency to avoid it by running away. Others let the disappointment occur just to have something to argue about or throw in the person's face.

God is the ultimate hero and He is able to be trusted with anything. He is strong enough and big enough to help us overcome anything. He allows us to walk to problems and then take us through them to see the victory.

GOD THE COMFORTER

According to *John* 14:16 (KJV), "And I will pray the Father, and he shall give you another Comforter, that he may abide with you forever." But Jesus did not leave us without help. He went on to say, "I will not leave you comfortless: I will come to you" (John 14:18 KJV). According to John 14:26 (NKJV), "But the Helper, the Holy Spirit, whom the Father will send in my name, He shall teach you all things, and bring all things to your remembrance, all things to you." *Jehovah Roi* means the God of all Comfort. *Jehovah Rohi* is the Lord is my Shepherd (Psalm 23:1), and *Jehovah Nacham* means the Lord is my Comforter (Isaiah 51:11–12, 66:12–13). The Holy Spirit is the third part of the Godhead or the Trinity. The Comforter Jesus Christ refers to is called the Holy Spirit, which comes to bring peace and tranquility during an unsettling situation. During times of sorrow the Comforter brings joy and happiness. When a person feels abandoned and he or she feels alone and despair starts to settle in his or her life, it is very hard to reach that individual. It takes prayer and an understanding advocate to step in and heal that person from the hurt. With God all things are possible. You will need to connect with God by giving your life to Christ and allow the Holy Spirit to come in and comfort you. You can find relief within if you throw up your hands and surrender your life to Christ and allow the Holy Spirit to caress you. It takes the saturation of the Holy Spirit to be able to endure and overcome such pain. The day of forgiveness and the ability to forget the things your parent said and did or didn't do during your childhood will soon be forgotten. You may say, "It's more easily said than done." You can forgive, but can you really forget the things of your past because somehow, somewhere it will come up again? Then how will you respond to the situation? It starts with accepting Christ in your life, and the Holy Spirit will come in if you want to be set free. The Holy Spirit will teach you how. It will allow you to respond responsibly to the things of your past. It will allow you to have joy despite the fact that others are trying to bring you down about your father. God will wrap you in the cradle of His arms and send the Holy Spirit to be there with you when people say things like, "Hey, I remember your father. He was a drunk." Or "Your father was mean, and he used to beat you." These reminders are hurtful for a child to hear, but even more so for an adult.

THE WONDERFUL COUNSELOR

A good father advises and counsels his children during their upbringing. A father teaches his child right from wrong and how to handle certain things in life. Young boys learn about cars and sports from their fathers. They also receive firsthand information about girls from their father. A father is able to mold and guide a child in the right direction. When a parent tells a child he or she is nothing and will never be anything or stoops to name calling, such as stupid, fool, and crazy, this leaves a long-lasting effect on a child's life. The child internalizes the message from his or her childhood and eventually acts out from the parent's name-calling in his or her adult life. If a child receives this type of message, it makes the child feel like he or she is worthless. The child learns to reach out to others, sometimes inappropriately, to release the hurt and pain.

God is able to resolve any problems if you let Him in. He can send a spiritual father in the adult child's life. The spiritual father can take the person by the hand and make the adult feel great about him/herself. Through spiritual guidance and positive counseling, the person is made to think and feel that he or she can do all things through Christ Jesus. The spiritual father is able to remind the child that he or she is somebody special because God loves him or her. The key to turning a warped mind into a mind of self-confidence and determination is to let the person know that the meaningless and non-significant person he or she was always told as a child is not the person he or she is now.

Sometimes when a family is not in harmony, they seek counseling to unite the family. The counseling can come from a therapist, psychologist, or someone from the ministry. It is a family's choice to have someone who does not have a genuine interest in the family or someone who is not associated with the family to talk with to gather insight and directions. It is important to have someone to listen during times of trouble and conflict in the home to help bring the family to an understanding that there is a need for resolution. Children often need someone to talk to whenever the parent is not available. When a child starts to show signs of trouble, it is best to call on an expert who specializes in this field. Child therapists have a way to reach out to troubled children and get to the root of the matter. They know how to pull the honesty out of situations and get the dialogue started. It's good to have someone to talk to and listen to you who has an objective mind. But it also comes with a fee to see a professional. A professional charges by the hour, and most of the time they require several sessions to "fix" the problem. The amount of time and money it takes to sit at a therapist's office can be directed to family meetings and family time, which can be facilitated by the leader of the family.

It is important that the child receives the lesson learned through the chastisement and not scolding them to make them feel bad. There is a big difference between counseling a child and scolding a child. Counseling can teach a person a lesson that can rationally impact his or her life. Scolding a person can only generate fear which impacts a child's life. Although it is understood that children do need to be chastised for their wrongdoings, parents must keep in mind that when a child is scolded, there is a sense of resentment placed upon the child towards the father. The appropriate structure and guidance is established through counseling. Fathers are known to be the go-to parent for disciplinary action because they provide the dominant and firm personality. Often times when a child does something wrong, the mom tells the child, "Just wait until your father gets home" or "I'ma tell your daddy when he gets home." The anticipation and the wait make a child wonder what might happen and know there will be a punishment ahead. Many times the talking alone provides a feeling of guilt that no beating can ever bring. It lets the child know that he or she did something that disappointed the parents and it should not happen again. Parents are not to keep bringing up the wrongness of the child and make a child feel he or she is a "bad" person. The child will have a difficult time growing from the situation if he or she is constantly reminded of his or her flaws. If Jesus is able to forgive us, then why can't parents?

Professional counseling and spiritual counseling are similar and yet different. Some of the situations may be different, but the technique may be the same. Both have a common goal involved, which is to help people overcome their problems and reach a positive outcome by finding the meaning and joy in life. There may be more of a principle relationship involved in spiritual counseling, especially if it is with your pastor or minister. Spiritual counseling distinctly involves the spiritual dimension, and it is guided by the biblical truths. This form of counseling is focused on seeking God's will in a person's life. It is the path and direction that a person wants to see him/herself travel in life with God as their navigator. At any rate, both types of counseling are valuable to help direct a person to live a healthy and well-adjusted life mentally and emotionally.

God, the Father has a way of counseling His children. He lets us know of our mistakes. God speaks to His children during our quiet time with Him, and He is a great listener too. You can talk to God as if you are talking to the person next to you, because He is real. But we must know the voice of God. When we concentrate on Him and rid ourselves from distractions, His Spirit becomes present in our darkest hour. When we get into our secret place and allow our hearts to be connected to God, He shows up through the Holy Spirit. And He won't tell your business to anyone.

God gets our attention through prayer, pastors, and His holy word. When God gets our attention, He gives us the free will to choose righteousness or evil. If we choose righteousness, then we must repent of our sins and never fall into the sin again. God is a forgiving God. He forgives us time after time when we fall. "For all have sinned, and come short of the glory of God" (Romans 3:23KJV).

Communication is the key. It takes having a spiritual communication with the almighty Father through prayer and fasting to be connected with Him. It is a process, yet a simple one. In some ways the process of spiritual communication is compared to planting a tree. When you plant a tree, you must first find your garden site, prepare your soil, then plant your seed and expect your harvest. Well, when you have a spiritual communication with God, you must first establish your secret place, then prepare your heart and mind to focus on God, then put your petition before God and look for your request to manifest. And as with all plants, it must be watered and nurtured. Just as through the understanding of the word of God, we must be nurtured as well. Jeremiah 17:7–8 lets us know that we are blessed because, "Blessed is the man that trust in the LORD, and whose hope the LORD is. For he shall be as a tree planted by the waters, and that spread out her roots by the river, and shall not see when heat cometh, but her leaf shall be green; and shall not be careful in the year of drought, neither shall cease from yielding fruit" (KJV).

The consequences are imaginable if we refuse to repent and remain in sin. As merciful as God is, He is also a God that does not like sin. He tells us in His word, "For the wages of sin is death, but the gift of God is eternal life through Christ Jesus" (Romans 6:23 KJV). God wants us to have eternal life. We have the free will to choose life while we live on this earth. He counsels us about showing love and how we must follow the same principles set forth by Jesus Christ so we can have the chance of eternal life to reign forever with Him in His kingdom.

"For unto us a child is born, unto us a son is given: and the government shall be upon his shoulder: and his name shall be called Wonderful, Counselor, The mighty God, The everlasting Father, The Prince of Peace" (Isaiah 9:6 KJV).

LOVE DON'T LIVE HERE ANYMORE

The Bible tells us that God is a God of love. But what happens when there's no love in the home? Imagine the absence of the father; the sole provider in the home has left. The family begins to feel a sense of loss, anger, and hurt. It is compared to the death of a significant loved one. When love no longer lives in the home anymore, it's similar to the feelings of the grieving process. When you take the letter e from the word dead, which represents the emptiness that a family experiences after losing their dad, we are left with a living person called dad. The departure of the dad, however it may occur, leaves the family empty and void. Yet, this is only a theory.

According to psychologists, there are five stages when someone suffers a loss and goes through the grieving process. Keep in mind that all people grieve differently. Some people will wear their emotions on their sleeve and be outwardly emotional. Others will experience their grief internally and may not cry. You should not judge how a person experiences grief, as each person will experience it differently. The stages are: 1) denial and isolation, 2) anger, 3) bargaining, 4) depression, and 5) acceptance. During the isolation and denial phase when a person loses a loved one, the person is in disbelief and withdrawn, and sometimes he or she tries to stay away from others, hoping the feeling will go away. And then the anger comes, hating everything about the person or hating the being that caused the death. Sometimes the person scorned even resents God and questions why this is happening to him or her. Then there is the bargaining with God and pleading with Him to make everything all right. You begin to tell Him that if He makes everything all right then you will do something in return. As time goes on, depression starts to settle in. Sadness and despair develop, along with the need to just have a pity party and cry. The feeling of depression lasts as long as the person dwells in his or her self-absorbed misery. Then you finally face the acceptance stage. You start to come to grips with what has happened and have the attitude that life goes on.

But sometimes the father leaving makes things better, especially when there is much arguing in the family between the father and mother. A child growing up in an environment filled with fussing and fighting is not healthy and has a long-lasting affect on the child as an adult. The parents have allowed the door to open for the enemy to come into the home and overshadow the love with hate. The togetherness causes separation, and the child becomes confused and isolated. The child starts to have trouble in school and his or her social life. Time and time again, when children come from disturbed homes, they don't know any other way to function. These children grow up demonstrating the same behavior as seen during their childhood, unless they allow God to enter into their lives. It is important that the father molds and sets the tone in the family with a loving, nurturing spirit—the kind of spirit that God himself demonstrates. The family must learn to function as a network. God is the power source, which feeds into the father, who is the receptor. The father receives the instructions from God, and he then releases that energy to his family. This energy works in a positive manner, and the outcome is successful. If the father ejects negative energy, the family will fall apart, and obviously this power is not of God. This is the reason God must be in the midst of the family in order for the family to prosper.

God is the key that unlocks the door to spiritual bondage. When love is taken from the home and especially the one who brings the love, you only have bitterness and anger left. The joy has left, and all you have are memories of yesterdays. The future does not look so bright, and the present is dull as well. You go through life doing the daily motions, thinking this is how it will be. God lets us know that trouble doesn't last always. We should not let our hearts worry about the things of tomorrow. We must believe in God and His Holy Spirit and rest assured that He will be our comforter. We have to first welcome Him in our hearts and then in our homes in order for Him to work in our lives.

If there are times when you feel broken and incomplete, the Lord is able to complete you. He can make you whole again. When all the happiness is gone in the home, the feeling of loneliness and heartache sets in, and you feel that no one cares. Just know that God cares. He can turn the sorrow into joy and the stormy nights into sunny mornings. Weeping may endure for a night, but joy comes in the morning. Each person's morning is determined by his or her faith. The power of love can be found again through the power of forgiveness. You can be set free from the hurt and heartache if you allow yourself to be endowed with the power of the Holy Ghost. The secret is not allowing the offender to continue having control of the matter and just forgive and be willing to mend the broken pieces. Matthew 6:14–15 teaches us how to let go of the hate through the power of forgiveness. It is the antidote to heal all scornful hearts. Holding on to something terrible for years and years will keep you from moving forward in life. It keeps you from growing healthy, emotionally and spiritually. That same unhealthy emotion will soon contaminate others who may become involved with you. Learning to let go of the past and the hurt that was caused by the pain of the father who abandoned you is the right thing that God the Father wants us to do. The power of forgiveness through God's love and comfort can bring us out of that burden of hatred and bitterness. When we learn to break the umbilical cord that leads to the turmoil from our past, then we can move forward to the process of forgiveness. We hinder our ability to experience true love because we carry so much baggage from our past. It takes first accepting the fact that your heart has been broken and then following the steps to do something about it. Love can be restored and dwell in our lives if we only acknowledge the hurt and the person who had hurt us. Then we can see the joy in our lives once again. It takes the acceptance of the Holy Spirit for you to allow your feelings to be processed. But the process does not happen instantaneously. It takes great strength and commitment to be able to let go of things others have done to you. It is obvious that when God steps in to comfort you, then everything is bound to work out for the good. He is a good God, and He never fails us and will never leave us. The Comforter, which is the Holy Spirit, is offered to us, only if we accept it. With the Holy Spirit, we learn to forgive others, even our absent father, as we expect our heavenly Father to forgive us. We have to surrender our all to Christ and allow the Holy Spirit to do its work.

Sometimes in life a loved one you cherish dearly meets their death. You don't understand why God plucked that flower from your family circle garden. There is a reason why God allows things to happen, and we need to trust that God knows what He is doing. Even though you know you must go on with life trusting Him, it is hard to face and go on. Everything starts to come at you all at once, and you start to feel like you are suffocating. You don't know how you can possibly go on. Each day grows effortless, and some days it's hard to get up in the morning. You find yourself balled up, crying like a little baby. This is the time when you need the strong arms of God to comfort you and raise you up and give you the air to breathe again. Ask Him to give you *CPR* (*C*ourage to *P*ress *R*egardless) so you can do His will despite the circumstance and despite what has gotten your spirits down. He can give you the courage to press against your tears regardless of how the enemy may try to keep you feeling depressed. The tears can turn into laughter, and then soon you will forget why you were crying in the first place. And know that crying is a remedy for sorrow. Some people find it difficult to cry in the presence of others. For some this is a sign of weakness, and so many of us have been conditioned in our childhood not to cry, to be strong. It is believed that shedding tears is a healthy way to release the stress in life. So it's okay to cry. God hears our cry, and He sees our tears. It relieves the pain and the heavy burdens that have been placed on our souls and minds. He sends the Holy Spirit to wrap us in the bosom of His care. God through the Holy Spirit provides us with comfort. He comforts us through all our troubles so we can comfort others. When others are troubled, we will be able to give them the same comfort God has given us (2 Corinthians 1:4). Because God cares for us, He provides us relief through times of trouble. "The Lord is our refuge, for in the day of trouble, he will keep us safe in his dwelling; he will hide us in the shelter of his sacred tent and set us high upon a rock" (Psalm 27:5 NIV). When you are feeling at your lowest point, the Holy Spirit brings peace and joy. Jesus Christ went away to be with His Father, but before He ascended to heaven He said, "Peace I leave with you, My peace I give to you; not as the world gives do I give to you. Let not your heart be troubled, neither let it be afraid. I am going away and coming back to you. If you loved Me, you would rejoice because I said, I am going to the Father, for My Father is greater than I" (John 14:27–28 NKJV). When Christ reminded His disciples that He was going to leave the Holy Spirit as a comforter, He was also letting us know we have access to the Holy Spirit, and by calling on the name of Jesus, we can activate the Holy Spirit. Mankind must learn to cover himself with the word as a person would wrap himself with a blanket for comfort.

God is able to comfort us when we feel alone and even lonely. He can be that confidant and more than a friend, that husband, that wife and companion when we feel like we have no one. The love God provides is eternal and will never end. It is man's love that sometimes ends. God's love is unconditional. He loves us despite of our flaws. Answer this question: Why is it so hard for some people to love? It's hard to love others when they do not want to be loved. Some people may say they want love, but they don't know how to obtain love because of the pain in their past. What is this love thing actually all about? Can we honestly say we love someone and really mean it? And what is love? Although love is just a four-letter word, it has a powerful meaning, and there are many characteristics of love. We know that love can be an emotional word, but it is also an action word. Love is giving and receiving. So you have to give love to be loved, and you have to be willing to receive love if you want to be loved. For example, if a person gives you something from the heart in love, the recipient would need to receive it in love and not turn it down. Therefore, God gave His

Son, Jesus, to the world out of love, and Jesus died on the cross out of love. We should accept Him out of love and give up sin because of love. And love is not vain or boastful. When you do something for someone, it's not for the giver to brag about the act in order to gain glory. Love is kind and gentle and beautiful. It reveals itself in a good way. Love and truth are companions, so love will never seek to be away from the truth. Sometimes love is used to teach a lesson, to discipline someone. In this case it can be a challenge because love is used to direct someone to make the right decision. Some call it "tough love." This means sometimes you have to be tough with the love or you have to make tough decisions while showing love to someone so he or she can make a change and grow up.

For you to experience the characteristics of love, you have to be able to find love within yourself. In order to love someone, you have to first have love for yourself and then adopt the love of God.

ALL GROWN UP NOW

When you entered adulthood, hopefully you learned to be more mature and responsible about life. It's a developmental stage in your life where you learned to let go of the bad things of your childhood. You have learned to put away those childish things, and you learn to cope with life much better. Things have become much easier since growing up in a household that made you either love or hate your father or you felt all alone. And even if you were surrounded by loved ones, you still felt alone. But now in your adult life, you know you are not alone. You are now grown up. You have the comfort of God, and you know His voice. He talks and walks with you to let you know He got you. He lets you know you are not having a mental breakdown when you hear His voice because He won't allow you to fall. It's not a breakdown, yet it's a breakthrough from the suffering caused in your childhood. You may have been put down, let down, and counted out. People, even your closest friends, think you are crazy or that you should have lost your mind. The enemy tried to take you out, but God said not so.

So you are all grown up now. You have managed to forget those things which are behind you and are looking forward to those things before you. You are pressing toward the mark, stepping one step at a time and believing that God is with you every step of the way. You are no longer receiving the breast milk that you were nurtured with as a child. The feeling of pity and blaming others no longer fills your belly. There is no more hurt and resentment to eat up your flesh. You can now love, and one day as a parent you will teach your own child(ren) the true meaning of love, which is the love of God. You have allowed the peace of God to surpass your soul to create a new and improved you. The absence of your natural father no longer affects you because you now realize that your heavenly Father has been with you the entire time waiting for you to accept Him. He has been waiting with His arms wide open, ready to wrap them around you. You have let your Daddy know He is home! He is home! He is home! It's time to welcome Him into your heart and walk into the path of righteousness.

You are all grown up. You should not fear or worry about what may happen or what might be said. You have nothing to fear because the Lord is your light and your salvation. He is the strength of your life. Why should you be afraid? And if you feel you have missed something in your life, keep your head lifted to the sky in search of a rainbow of truth, where each color represents the episodes you have traveled in your lifetime. Regardless of whether your rainbow consists of dark and dreary colors when focusing on the dark days from your past, you can cast your rainbow toward the Son, who is Jesus Christ. You will see your rainbow beginning to become brighter. The God of truth will walk you in the path of righteousness. There you will find peace and happiness, which is His reward.

You are all grown up. You are now faced with the person who did you wrong and abandoned you for so many years. You rehearsed over and over what you might do, and now the time has come. You are at a crossroad. What do you say? What do you do? You feel like embracing him because the God in you wants you to. You don't walk past him because that's what the enemy would have you to do. The bittersweet moment has arrived. That inner child who once lived in you, who prepared you to let out all the pain when confronted with this person, has now put you in a forgiven place in life. Just remember the person who wronged you does not know what to say either, because he knows he wronged you. It is up to you to be the bigger person and step up. You are in a position to greet this person with love and kindness and say hi rather than, "I don't know you." You can ask this person what he needs instead of what he hasn't done for you. You can give him a hug instead of walking away. You can hold a conversation and invite him over to your house one day; instead of saying, "I don't want to see you anymore". There is a positive force that wills you to be kind and have a spirit of forgiveness. The force outweighs all the ugly hurt on the inside. It may be hard sometimes to treat a person with such humility when he has not shown you any love. But the Christ in you will allow you to do the right thing because you are a new creature. The old you had passed, and you are now all grown up.

So now you know your father because you know God. You must take the time away from your busy schedule to give God thanks. As an adult you have the opportunity to visit Him instead of Him visiting you. You might think you know who your Father is now, and you don't need a blood test to tell you so. But there is something more each day we can learn about Him and from Him. You must find your secret private space and dwell in His presence. Schedule a meeting with Him, and allow Him to be ushered into your life.

Many times we make time for our jobs and other affairs and find ourselves missing our time with God. Why not make time for Him? He should be the CEO (chief everlasting officer) of your life. He has given us life and much more because He is our Father, provider, protector, and comforter. So don't you quit on Him because He will not quit on you. God's arms have held you for so long, providing you with comfort and protection. Allow Him to continue to hold you even while you are all grown up. We must remain close to Him even more now than ever because we need our Daddy to be there for us to defeat the enemy. We must know the word for ourselves and remember the spiritual things we learned to guide us along the way. In the natural, remember when your parent was not always around you and you had to decide right from wrong. Well, the day will come when the presence of the Lord will no longer be around on this earth, and you will be forced to choose between good and evil, and you will need to choose wisely. But within the word of God there is a hiding place, and you must keep the word hidden in your heart as your comforter and use it as your weapon to fight the enemy.

When you are wrapped in the arms of God, you are guided by the touch of His fingers, you are comforted by His hands, and you are strengthened by the power of God's arms. It's like when a newborn baby is wrapped up so tight in a pretty pink or blue blanket. The baby is kept warm and all snuggled up, thinking he or she is still protected in the mother's stomach. They appear so innocent and precious to the sight of the parent and the family. The baby is handled with care because he or she is so fragile. The baby is soothed by the parents' touch, comforted by the mother's love, and guarded by the father's strength. When you are wrapped in the arms of God, it is like having a gift box wrapped up so tight and decorated so pretty. If the gift is fragile, you want to protect it. The receiver has no idea what to expect. And when the gift is opened, there is usually something precious inside.

Sometimes it is something you think you might not need, but you will someday. You will cherish it as being near and dear to your heart. God sees us as being near and dear to His heart. He sees us as being special because He has no respecter of persons. God shows no partiality with His children. He gives us want we need, and sometimes He gives us the things we want. There is a saying that is used in church: "He may not come when we want Him, but He is right on time." We all are important to Him, and He sees us as unique individuals with our own personality. God desires us to have a righteous personality, just as He has. And through His Son Jesus Christ we can achieve His plan that He has for us. For God's plan is simple. We live according to His word and love one another. If people find this plan so hard to do, then the day will come when they will miss out on a life of eternity with our Father. Allow the Lord to take over your life, your heart, and your soul. Let Him wrap His loving arms around you today. May the peace of God keep you now and forever more!

Printed in the United States
By Bookmasters